The SIMPLE Path

The simple path to simplify your life

Jamie E Stilwill & Kristine K Nicholson

Simplify 98038, LLC

Simplify 98038 LLC
27177 185th Ave SE Ste 111 – 233
Covington, WA 98042

Library of Congress Control Number: 2025911287
ISBN: 9798998971181
USA

Acknowledgements

We would like to acknowledge all of our friends, family, and
colleagues who have contributed to our learning, inspiration,
and encouraging us along the way.

A special thank you to Audra Wilson, Jennifer Haury, Shelly
Connors, and Jenn Alvin for helping us to get through the last
mile of this journey.

The SIMPLE Path

The simple path to simplify your life

Start with you

Identify what is important

Manage the chaos

Pick your improvement

Learn from it

Employ and Enjoy

The SIMPLE Path
is a new and simple
framework for improvement
developed by
Jamie E Stilwill and Kristine K Nicholson

Contents

Introduction

Who this book is for and how to use it.

This book is for you if you want to make things better and easier. But here's the truth: you are the key ingredient; nothing works without you. The SIMPLE Path is your path, and it all starts with you...so buckle up!

The SIMPLE Path will help you no matter what role you have: leader, employee, business owner, parent, partner, volunteer, community organizer, influencer, etc. If you resonate with any of the statements below, The SIMPLE Path is for you.

- I want change, but I don't know where to start.
- I get frustrated when I think people don't do things the way they "should."
- I'm not sure why I do the things I do.
- I've been told I am not doing enough.
- I do a lot and I am not making progress on anything.
- I know what I want, but I don't know how to get there.

This book contains not only the steps, but also tangible ways that you can practice, apply, and grow.

How to use this book

Start with the assessment. This will give you a baseline of where you are starting The SIMPLE Path.

The SIMPLE Path is designed sequentially and *Start with you* is the first step.

- If you are looking to use this as a guide to work through solving a particular problem or a specific project, we recommend going through the guide in a sequential order.
- If you are looking to grow in specific areas, you are welcome to bounce around to the different topics in whatever order of growth you prioritize.

Regularly update The SIMPLE Path assessment.

- As you learn, develop, and grow, your answers will change. As you learn more and practice, re-assessing will help give you new places to focus.

Caution: Be careful not to focus on too much at once.

- When too many changes are done simultaneously, it's challenging to pinpoint which change is working. Some people may choose to focus on one behavior; some may choose to focus on all the behaviors in a particular path. Whichever method you choose, give yourself some time to focus and grow before moving on. It takes time to build a habit. You may have to try a few different things before finding the sweet spot for you.

Ask for help: You can get help along the way.

- Visit https://the-simple-path.com to learn more and inquire about:
  - Consultations for businesses and individuals
  - One-on-one individual coaching
  - Facilitated group workshops and retreats
  - Supplemental Tools and Resources

The SIMPLE Path Assessment

Before you start, you need to know where to begin.

The SIMPLE Path assessment can help you understand your strengths and growth opportunities which will help you prioritize your learnings. Your scores will change as you learn more and will sometimes go down. That is okay. We encourage you to retake this assessment regularly so you can see your growth and reprioritize your learnings. (There are extra assessments in the last section of this book, starting on page 71.) It is not an expectation to be at *Always* for everything, but following The SIMPLE Path will get you closer.

The SIMPLE Path Assessment

Rate yourself on the behaviors below.

0: Never	1: Rarely	2: Sometimes	3: Always

The SIMPLE Path	Behaviors	0	1	2	3
Start with you	I have a growth mindset.				
	I seek to understand.				
	I embrace change.				
Identify what is important	I know why my work matters.				
	I have a clear and concise direction.				
	I know who is impacted.				
Manage the chaos	I am able to eliminate distractions.				
	I create, communicate, and enforce boundaries.				
	I prioritize my attention on what I can control.				
Pick your improvement	I reduce complexity in everything I do.				
	I use evidence and data to understand what is really happening.				
	I consider the people who are impacted by the work.				

Learn from it	I avoid assumptions.				
	I embrace failure.				
	I use my learnings to implement or try again.				
Employ and enjoy	I communicate changes to those impacted.				
	I employ ways to make new ideas stick.				
	I celebrate the wins.				

Reflection:

- What sections are your strengths (highest scores)? How do you demonstrate these behaviors?

- What sections are your opportunities (lowest scores)? What section do you feel growth will make a difference in your life right now?

- What surprised you as you reflected on The SIMPLE Path and behaviors?

Start with you

Prepare yourself for growth, understanding, and change.

It all starts with you. Before looking at anything else, we need to look at ourselves. The way you approach and respond to situations is your truth, the foundation for how things are. If we continue to approach things the way we always have, nothing will change. Einstein is quoted as saying, "The definition of insanity is doing the same thing over and over again and expecting different results." It's easy to say that other people need to do this or that, but you only have control over your own actions. As you commit to a personal change, you will see an impact on the culture around you.

We tend to do our routines as habits and don't ask ourselves why we are doing what we're doing. It's just the way that things have always been done. **The Story of the Pot Roast** is a parable that has been shared in many publications.

> A young woman was hosting a dinner party for her friends and served a delicious pot roast. One of her friends enjoyed it so much that she asked for the recipe, and the young woman wrote it down for her.
>
> Upon looking over the recipe, her friend inquired, "Why do you cut both ends off the roast before it is prepared and put in the pan?" The young woman replied, "I don't know. I cut the ends off because I learned this recipe from my dad and that was the way he had always done it."

Her friend's question got the young woman thinking and so the next day she called her dad to ask him: *"Dad when we make pot roast, why do we cut the ends off?"* Her dad quickly replied, *"That's how your grandma always did it and I learned the recipe from her."*

Now the young woman was really curious, so she called her elderly grandma and asked her the same question: "Grandma, I often make the pot roast recipe that I learned from dad and he learned from you. Why do you cut the ends off the roast before you prepare it?"

The grandmother thought for a while, since it had been years since she made the roast herself, and then replied, "I cut them off because the roast was always bigger than the pan I had back then. I had to cut the ends off to make it fit."

We enjoy this parable because it is so true for many of our actions. We rarely think why we do things anymore. We have been doing things for so long we don't challenge the status quo and ask ourselves why we act a certain way or make the decisions we make. The SIMPLE Path requires a different mindset. We must disrupt this thinking. We have to stop and ask questions. Why do we do things the way we have always done them? Why do we treat people the way we do? If we want a different outcome, it is up to no one but ourselves to change.

There are no hacks. It's you against you. This has to be in you. Something in you has to wake up. And usually, the only person that can wake it up is you. ~ David Goggins

What does "Start with you" look like for you?
Write down or draw your thoughts. What do you see in the mirror?

Start with you: activity to progress

Behavior: I have a growth mindset.

How to Progress:

- **Reflect every day.** What went really well? What could have been better?
- **Apply a beginner's mind.** Challenge the status quo (what you always do just because) and look for new and novel ways of doing things.
- **Proactive thinking.** Be in the driver's seat. You get to decide every decision you make and every perspective you take. When you feel like reacting, PAUSE. Reflect on what actions are in alignment with your values.

What will I commit to doing?

How can I start today?

Behavior: I seek to understand.

  How to Progress:

- **Start with positive intentions.** Look at the facts from a positive perspective.
- **Challenge your assumptions.** Disrupt your thinking. Stop and question why you are doing things the way you have always done them and why you treat people the way you do.
- **Be curious.** Ask questions. Gather other's opinions, perspectives, and their approaches to certain things. There are potential new answers and solutions to problems hidden in other people's thinking. Expand your sources to gain more diverse insight.

What will I commit to doing?

How can I start today?

Behavior: I embrace change.

How to Progress:

- **Try something new.** Take a different route to work, read a book in a genre you usually avoid, or brush your teeth with the other hand. Each of these activities opens your mind to new points of view.
- **Look for easier ways to do things.** Do you get value from every action you take? Do you get value from everything you use? If you don't, try cutting those out to make it easier. Start small.
- **Understand your resistance.** It is normal to resist change, people have a natural instinct to say, "Heck no!" Questions to understand the root of your resistance: Is it because I don't like the person asking me to change? Do I understand the change? Am I afraid to lose something? Do I think it will fail?

What will I commit to doing?

How can I start today?

Identify what is important
Create clear priorities that matter.

We are pulled in many directions and have many people vying for our attention. Our employees, bosses, friends, family, and business relationships all have priorities...and they don't always align. It is important to be clear about what is important to you. We cannot depend on others to tell us what is important, because we will be tempted to focus on what is important to them and ignore what is important to ourselves. This can cause feelings of resentment. However, the sweet spot is when you are able to create alignment and move in the same direction together. Identifying what is important gives you the ability to focus on a clear direction and you will know for whom and why it all matters.

Have you ever been on a project or a team where you all had good intentions to make things better, but everyone had different ideas on what that was? When we want to get better, but are unable to define what "that" is, we go in all different directions. Lacking clarity and alignment on purpose and goals can be why relationships fall apart. Sadly, we see people drift apart because they lose sight of what is important or because they were really never in sync in the first place.

A simple activity you can try with a group of colleagues, friends, or family members to illustrate the importance of having a clear direction can be accomplished with a stick. Ask everyone who is part of the group to put one hand on the stick, face away from it, and try to start walking. What happened? The group didn't get anywhere. Everyone went in different directions, which meant they went nowhere.

Reset and ask the group to put one hand on the stick and go towards the door. What do you think happened this time? They were able to move forward together.

Replace the stick with any situation. Where do people go? This activity can help teams recognize they have different priorities in values, relationships, and work which leads people to go in many different directions. Finding a common direction can leverage differences to move forward as individuals together.

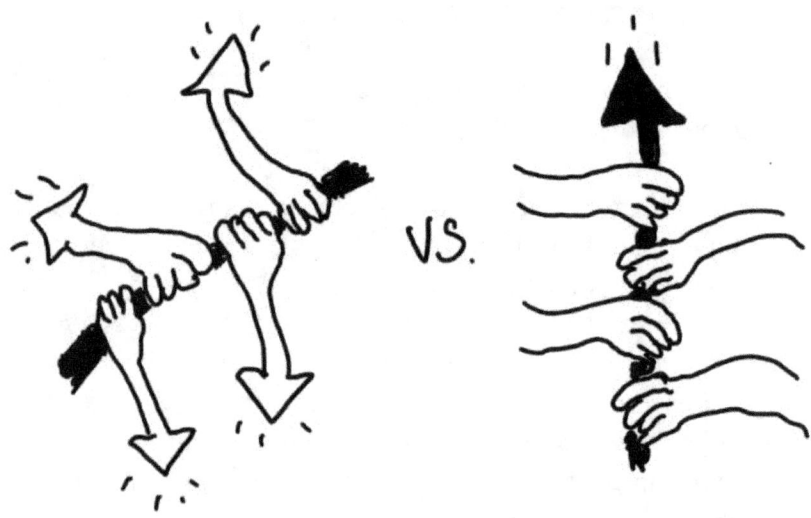

What does "Identify what is important" look like for you? *Write down or draw your thoughts. What is important to you?*

Identify what is important: activity to progress

Behavior: I know why my work matters.

How to Progress:

- **Create a mission statement.** Defines what you do, who you do it for, how you do it, and why it matters. This doesn't have to be lofty or perfect. This is simply to get you to think about why your work matters.
- **Create a vision statement.** What impact do you see for yourself, your business, your work in the future? What would you like to achieve for you and your customers?
- **Share your elevator pitch.** Create an elevator pitch, create a 20 second or less elevator pitch, that clearly and concisely articulates the *why* behind what you are doing and the value your work creates. The more you practice your elevator pitch, the clearer and more concise you will become. Hint: Include your mission and vision statements.
- **Be intentional.** Make sure that your actions align with your purpose. When you don't know why you are doing something, pause and ask yourself if you should be doing it.

What will I commit to doing?

How can I start today?

Behavior: I have a clear and concise direction.

How to Progress:

- **Write Specific, Measurable, Achievable, Relevant, Timebound, Inclusive, and Equitable (SMARTIE) goals and limit yourself to no more than 5.** When writing goals use the following framework:
  - *Verb – What you are wanting to do*
  - *Noun - What you are measuring*
  - From *Current condition*
  - To *Goal measure*
  - By *Complete date*

  Example: Improve employee satisfaction scores from 3.75 to 4.50 by February 14, 2026.

- **Make your goals visible.** Post your goals where others can see them. Expectations are made clear when people are aware of them and if these are individual goals sharing them with others will help with accountability.

- **Review at least daily.** Make reviewing your goal daily a habit. This keeps your goal at the front of your mind. What you prioritize is what you spend your time on.

What will I commit to doing?

How can I start today?

Behavior: I know who is impacted.
How to Progress:
- **Identify who your customers are.** At the end of everything you do, there is someone this is for and that is the "customer." Is it for the benefit of you, your family, your colleague, your business partner?
- **Ask your customers what they want/need.** If you don't know what your customers want, go ask them. You may be doing more than what they need or providing something they may not want at all.
- **Understand who is involved.** Dissect who is involved in the work, who is impacted by the outcome, and consider who may be missing.

What will I commit to doing?

How can I start today?

Manage the chaos

Focus your energy using the MC Squares.

Managing the chaos helps to flick away everything except what matters and is within our control. We are not sacrificing anything; we are making choices based on how we prioritize things. The MC Squares listed below is a helpful tool to prioritize what matters and what is within our control.

E = MC Squares

Focus my energy on what matters and
what is within my control

It matters a lot and is not within my control.	**Focus here** It matters a lot and is within my control.
It doesn't matter and is not within my control.	It doesn't matter and is within my control.

It Matters

Within my **Control**

Sometimes our minds can feel like a snow globe after it is shaken, and the snow is everywhere. It is difficult to focus on anything. It feels like we're being pulled in a zillion different directions. There is way too much and focusing on anything becomes an obstacle. Then the snow starts to settle and things start to get clearer. Managing the chaos is getting that clarity. Clearing away the things that don't matter. Settling your thoughts and ideas so you can identify the ones you need to pay attention to.

There is a lot going on around world. While listening to the news is helpful to keep informed, it can be filled with sensationalized stories intended to rattle us. It is frustrating to be faced with so many things that we don't feel we can do anything about. It can force us into the drama triangle, a concept proposed by Stephen Karpman, whereas it is a pattern of dysfunction where people cycle through the roles of Victim, Persecutor, and Rescuer. As a victim, some people get stuck and can't do anything, unable to sleep because of the worry they have. As a persecutor, some people go to social media to vent and shout blame out to whomever will listen. As a rescuer, some people react and walk right into the fire without calling 911 first, putting themselves and others in danger as they get in the way. By being clear around what matters and what's in your control, you can get out of the drama triangle and move forward with purpose.

What does "Manage the chaos" look like for you?
Write down or draw your thoughts. Where should your energy go?

Manage the chaos: activity to progress

Behavior: I am able to eliminate distractions.
How to Progress:

- **Be present**. Practice focusing only on what is in front of you. If your mind starts to wander because of noises, people talking, emails popping up, or worry, consider ways to keep you present. Play lo-fi music or nature sounds, make what you are doing visual, close your email, give yourself grace as your mind wanders, but find your way back.

- **Focus on what you can influence.** Understand where your influences end and practice how you respond to experiences you cannot control. You are not the decision maker for everything, but you can always do something. For example, if Congress has a bill presented to them that you like, you do not get a vote if it gets passed or not. But you can call your congressperson and share your views.

- **Focus on one thing at a time.** When we are constantly switching tasks, we are less productive and are more likely to make a mistake. If you find yourself wanting to switch tasks, try taking a 3-5 minute break by stretching, getting a glass of water, going outside for a brief walk...then get back to it.

What will I commit to doing?

How can I start today?

Behavior: I create, communicate, and enforce boundaries.

How to Progress:

- **Create boundaries.** What do you consider okay and not okay for you to do or accept from others? You are not able to control other people's actions, but you can control how you respond. When something doesn't feel right or it's not aligned with your values, consider what your ideal outcome would be. What boundary can you create so that your actions align with your goals and values? What would the perfect situation look like? Identify when a boundary is needed, define it, communicate it, and then enforce it. "People treat you according to your boundaries" ~ Nedra Tawwab

- **Craft a boundary statement.** Describe the situation. Express your desired result and then state the consequence. Remember to respect other's boundaries too.
  "Choose discomfort over resentment" -Brené Brown. For example, a boundary could be needed when family calls to chat during work hours. The boundary could be defined as not answering phone calls from family members during business hours, unless it's an emergency which is when they call twice in a row. Then enforcing it by only answering when they call twice.

- **Create leader standard work.** Leader standard work is the visual management of reoccurring activities. Capture your daily, weekly, and monthly list of priorities. Identify the limits you establish for yourself, share them with others, and stick to them.

What will I commit to doing?

How can I start today?

Behavior: I prioritize my attention on what I can control.

How to Progress:

- **Complete the MC Squares Exercise.** Know what matters and understand what is within your control. Consider things your attention is being called to and plot them on the MC Squares pick chart. For things that matter to you a lot (Reference the section *Identify what's important*), place them toward the top of the chart. Then consider how much control you have over them. If it's not much control, it would be further left. If it is within your span of control, it would be further right. Then plot on the chart where the how much it matters and how much control you have intersect. The top right section is when things matter more and you have more control. This is a great place to prioritize your attention. This is where you spend your energy.

E = MC Squares

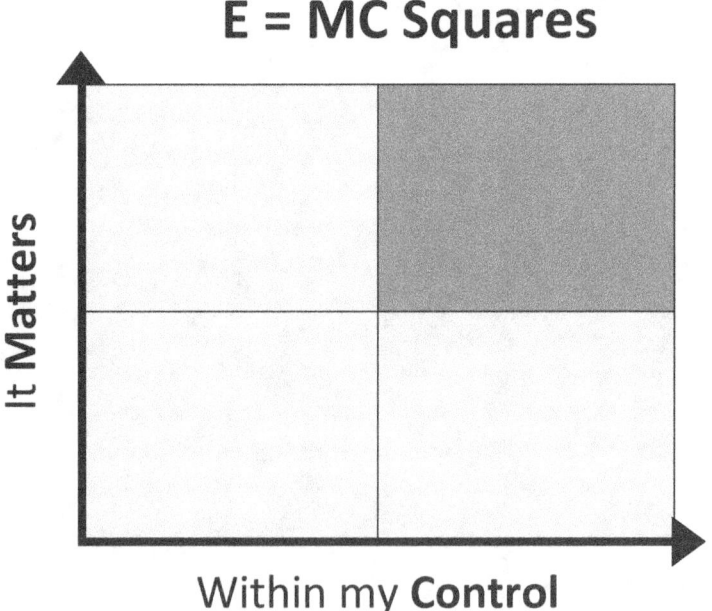

It Matters

Within my **Control**

What will I commit to doing?

How can I start today?

Pick your improvement
Make things better.

Improvement is simply to make things better. Improvements can happen on both large and small scales...and they all happen one little bit at a time. When you see people getting recognized for a giant improvement, it didn't happen all at once. There were many small trials and improvements that happened along the way.

When you implement, you are checking boxes and putting things in place that may not make it better. Improvement starts with understanding what is happening, creating a standard and consistent way of doing it, identifying what areas could be better, and testing little ways to try and make it better.

Someone once said, "Why are we spending time going over what is happening now? Don't you think our time would be better spent just creating the new process?" The initial reaction could be, "YES! Let's just focus on developing the solutions by ourselves."

Challenges arise when skipping to the solutions and doing them in isolation. Implementing what you develop may result in something different, but also have unanticipated problems and issues. People won't understand it when you don't involve them in the process.

You can try to complete it and make it to be what you believe is perfect. But when you roll out the solution to others, they discover issues you were never aware of.

There is a benefit to starting from the beginning, involving the people who do the work, and trying until things get better. Nietzsche is quoted as saying, "The end of a melody is not its goal: but nonetheless, had the melody not reached its end it would not have reached its goal either." Improvement is the melody. Improvement is the journey...and the outcomes are so much better.

What does "Pick your improvement" look like for you?
Write down or draw your thoughts. What does it mean to improve?

Pick your improvement: activity to progress

Behavior: I reduce complexity in everything I do.
How to Progress:

- **Capture your current state.** Map out a process. Identify in your current state where there is variation. Where steps are not clear? Where do things go wrong? Do you get complaints?
- **Develop a standard for one process.** Involve your team and make it as visual as possible.

Step	Description	Key Points
Starts with a verb and is under 10 words.	Description with pictures as needed of how to do the step.	Why the step is needed and what could happen if not done a specific way.

- **Measure what is important.** Create key performance indicators (KPIs) to measure. This can help you see how you are meeting your customers' expectations or show where some attention is needed.
- **Improve one thing at a time. Start small and see if it makes an impact.** If you change multiple variables at a time, how will you know if it made a difference?

What will you try?	What do you expect?	Try the thing	What happened?	What did you learn?

What will I commit to doing?

How can I start today?

Behavior: I use evidence and data to understand what is really happening.

How to Progress:

- **Collect data.** Collecting data helps us to understand if we have made a difference and gives us additional insight to make informed decisions. Ways to collect data: interviews, surveys, reports, observations, tallies, polls.
- **Challenge assumptions**. If you aren't 100% sure you know why, how, or what is happening, seek to find out more information.
- **Choose facts.** Don't think, go and see. Going to see the process helps us see what is really happening instead of what we think is happening. If you ask someone what they do, they will tell you what happens in the best way they know how. They may inadvertently miss sharing details because they are so used to it. The only way you can fully understand the process is to see it happen in real time.

What will I commit to doing?

How can I start today?

Behavior: I consider the people who are impacted by the work.

How to Progress:

- **Defer to expertise.** Involve the people who do the work in improvements.
- **Reframe failure.** When mistakes happen, reframe your thinking and try to figure out what in the process broke down instead of who made the mistake. Try to reframe instead of blaming people. People are only set up to succeed to the level of the systems they are working in.
- **Focus on the process rather than the outcome.** Even if the outcomes are great, if the process to get there has variation or requires an unrealistic amount of work and effort, it is not great. Focusing on the process can show the people who are impacted by the work that the time they are spending on the work is worthwhile.

What will I commit to doing?

How can I start today?

Learn from it

Reflect and reframe to move forward.

Learning is an underrated part of improving. Your mind tends to fill in gaps with stories that may or may not be true. Avoid assumptions so that your learnings are actual learnings that you can confidently move forward with. When we test and try new things we may not always succeed. It is ok to fail. Shifting the perspective on failure to be a learning opportunity will only create a safe space for future improvements. Failures are not a full stop, they provide us a chance to reevaluate, learn something, and decide what to do next.

We have all experienced failure. Maybe we didn't pass a test, tanked a presentation, shrunk a favorite sweater, or missed a deadline. Learning from failure often requires us to face difficult emotions like guilt or disappointment. Embracing those feelings and not letting them control us is key. The moment we reframe failure we will open ourselves up to innovation and exploration. When things don't go right, we can ask ourselves, "What did we learn?" When things do go right, we can then ask ourselves, "How do we do more of it and what did we learn?" When we focus more on learning, and less about succeeding and perfection, we are more likely to try new things even if we lack the certainty of the outcome. This is called continuous improvement. Failure isn't the end of the story. It's a plot twist.

What does "Learn from it" look like for you?
Write down or draw your thoughts. How will you reframe failure?

Learn from it: activity to progress

Behavior: I avoid assumptions.
How to Progress:

- **Collect data to inform my learning.** Stick to the facts. Find tangible details to work with. Do I know for a fact that this is true?" or "Do I have enough data/evidence to prove that this is the case?"
- **Add "because" after statements.** Seek out the rationale for your statement. If you're not sure, that is an opportunity to get some information. This is going well because <reason>. Hint – "because I think so" is a good indicator that a statement is an assumption. Understand the reasons for your thinking.

What will I commit to doing?

How can I start today?

Behavior: I embrace failure.

How to Progress:

- **Use "whoopsie" instead of "failure."** If "failure" is a barrier for you, call it something else. What is important is reducing the fear of failure, not what it's called. If it feels better for you to rename it as something else, do it!

- **Ask yourself, "What did I learn?"** When something fails, it does not mean that YOU are a failure. The thing you tried didn't work. You can reframe the failure as an opportunity to learn and inform what you do next.

- **Add talking about a failure to a recurring agenda or conversation.** When you are able to continue talking about failures, it normalizes them. Failures happen all the time by everyone. When we talk about failure as part of our normal conversations, it helps us to realize they don't only happen to us and they don't all cause massive destruction.

What will I commit to doing?

How can I start today?

Behavior: I use my learnings to implement or try again.
How to Progress:

- **Reflect on why things worked or didn't work.** This will help you know what to do more or less of.

- **Reflect on a rapid improvement**. Try a different way of putting a cup away from the dishwasher, reflect on what made it better or worse, and try again with the next cup. This is a simple way to practice rapid improvement. Remember to reflect so you can learn and try again right away.

- **Ask yourself, what did you learn from the last thing you tried?** When you want to try making something better, ask yourself what you tried the last time and what you learned. It's part of human nature to make things better, and we usually do things over and over....so what can you learn from the last time you tried to make it better? You did something and can leverage that information so you're not starting from scratch each time.

What will I commit to doing?

How can I start today?

Employ and enjoy

Spread the good stuff and celebrate.

It's not enough to develop an improvement, but you get to employ and enjoy too! Employing involves supporting people through the change so that you can all realize and enjoy the benefits!

Imagine implementing a new technology. Then the day it went live, you had to switch from the old technology to the new technology, with no overlap in between. The system worked, but not enough people knew how to use it, why the change was happening in the first place, and communications were missed because it was buried deep in their email. An idea or improvement is only good if it can be spread to those who need to do it. People need to want the change, know how to do it, have support to stick with it, and celebrate!

What does "Employ and enjoy" look like for you?
Write down or draw your thoughts. How will you support others through the change?

Employ and enjoy: activity to progress

Behavior: I communicate changes to those impacted.
How to Progress:

- **Inform those impacted by the change.** Change happens at the individual level. One communication method that works for one person may not work for others. Try multiple communication channels (email, text, conversation, signs, etc.) and make sure that whatever you are doing helps them become aware. This is not about what is convenient for you, this is about how they can receive the information to support the change you want to see.
- **Support people through change**. Share why the change is coming, manage resistance, give people the space to understand and learn how to do the change.

What will I commit to doing?

How can I start today?

Behavior: I employ ways to make new ideas stick.
How to Progress:

- **Make it easy.** Make the right work the easy work to do. When the new way of doing things is easier, and the old way is harder, it will stick. Consider habit stacking, a practice popularized by James Clear. Attaching what you want to be a new habit to something you already have a habit of doing.
- **Make it obvious.** Don't rely on memories that can fall back to previous habits. Make it visual and very obvious as a reminder to do the new thing.
- **Find an accountability buddy.** Don't do change alone. When you have someone else to encourage and support it helps you to keep going instead of giving up.

What will I commit to doing?

How can I start today?

Behavior: I celebrate the wins.

How to Progress:

- **Build in celebration.** Throughout and at the end of improvements pause to recognize your team's contributions. If you want improvements to continue, recognize the behaviors you want to see more of. Be specific and genuine. Not everything has to be a costly celebration. Sometimes a simple thank you is enough.
- **Make everyone part of the success.** You probably didn't do this alone, so share any accolades and recognition with others.
- **Show the data that demonstrates improvement.** Did your improvement save you 5 minutes of time? YES! Show that data.

What will I commit to doing?

How can I start today?

You made it!

You made it through The SIMPLE Path!

Start with you

Prepare yourself for growth, understanding, and change.

Identify what is important

Create clear priorities that matter.

Manage the chaos

Focus your energy using the MC Squares.

Pick your improvement

Make things better.

Learn from It

Reflect and reframe to move forward.

Employ and enjoy

Spread the good stuff and celebrate.

Whether you went through the whole journey sequentially, or skipped around to the parts you wanted to focus on, you have learned something. The SIMPLE Path is a journey that may feel a little bumpy at times. Give yourself grace as you try new ways of doing things. Regularly rinse and repeat through The SIMPLE Path. The more practice you have, the easier it will become.

At the very beginning of this guide, you probably took The SIMPLE Path Assessment. We encourage you to retake this assessment regularly so you can see your growth and reprioritize your learnings.

Go forth and keep it simple!

For additional support on your SIMPLE Path journey, visit https://the-simple-path.com or email us at info@the-simple-path.com to explore:
- Consultations for businesses and individuals
- One-on-one individual coaching
- Facilitated group workshops and retreats
- Supplemental Tools and Resources

We're here to walk alongside you—every step of the way.

The SIMPLE Path Assessment

Re-rate yourself on the behaviors below.

0: Never	1: Rarely	2: Sometimes	3: Always

The SIMPLE Path	Behaviors	0	1	2	3
Start with you	I have a growth mindset.				
	I seek to understand.				
	I embrace change.				
Identify what is important	I know why my work matters.				
	I have a clear and concise direction.				
	I know who is impacted.				
Manage the chaos	I am able to eliminate distractions.				
	I create, communicate, and enforce boundaries.				
	I prioritize my attention on what I can control.				
Pick your improvement	I reduce complexity in everything I do.				
	I use evidence and data to understand what is really happening.				
	I consider the people who are impacted by the work.				

Learn from it	I avoid assumptions.				
	I embrace failure.				
	I use my learnings to implement or try again.				
Employ and enjoy	I communicate changes to those impacted.				
	I employ ways to make new ideas stick.				
	I celebrate the wins.				

Reflection:

- What sections are your strengths (highest scores)? How do you demonstrate these behaviors?

- What sections are your opportunities (lowest scores)? What section do you feel growth will make a difference in your life right now?

- What surprised you as you reflected on The SIMPLE Path and behaviors?

- What will you do next?

Notes

Start with you

1. "The definition of insanity is doing the same thing over and over again and expecting different results." The original source of this quotation is unknown but is generally attributed to Albert Einstein.
2. "The Story of the Pot Roast" The original source of the story is unknown but different versions have been shared in many publications.
3. *"There are no hacks. It's you against you. This has to be in you. Something in you has to wake up. And usually, the only person that can wake it up is you."* This quote is widely attributed to David Goggins, former Navy SEAL and author of Can't Hurt Me (2018). Exact source unclear but consistent with his motivational style.

Manage the chaos

1. Karpman, Stephen B. Fairy Tales and Script Drama Analysis. Transactional Analysis Bulletin, Vol. 7, No. 26, 1968, pp. 39–43.
2. Tawwab, Nedra Glover. Set Boundaries, Find Peace: A Guide to Reclaiming Yourself. TarcherPerigee, 2021. p. 219.
3. Brown, Brené. Daring Greatly: How the Courage to Be Vulnerable Transforms the Way We Live, Love, Parent, and Lead. Gotham Books, 2012.

Pick your improvement

1. Nietzsche, Friedrich. *Human, All Too Human: A Book for Free Spirits*. Translated by R.J. Hollingdale, Cambridge University Press, 1996. Originally published 1878.

Employ and enjoy

1. Clear, James. *Atomic Habits: An Easy & Proven Way to Build Good Habits & Break Bad Ones.* Avery, 2018.

About the authors

Jamie E. Stilwill and Kristine K. Nicholson met in 2017 when they became colleagues. They heard frustrations from everyone: friends, family, coworkers, acquaintances, and business owners. They saw in each other a common desire and ability to break things down and simplify what appears to be seemingly complex. They wanted to create something that was simple enough to follow so that anyone could understand and improve whatever they wanted to. Their top two goals were to help people and have fun. As they brainstormed what this might look like, they kept going back to, "It has to be simple, Simple, SIMPLE." Which brought them to begin developing The SIMPLE Path in 2023.

Jamie E. Stilwill started her work with standards, improvements and making things simple in 2014. She grew into her consulting and leadership role in 2017, focusing more on supporting the growth and development of others and organizations. She earned her Bachelor of Science from Pacific

Lutheran University, and Master of Health Administration from the University of Washington, and has over a decade of process improvement and change management experience. Jamie has a passion for learning and sharing her knowledge with others. She has received certifications from Prosci, the Association of Change Management Professionals, PMI and is Lean Black Belt and Lean Six-Sigma Green Belt certified. Jamie has presented and connected with people through podcasts, webinars, conferences and trainings. She and her husband, Charlie, share their home in Maple Valley, Washington with two amazing children, Abby and Jackson and a lifetime collection of Disney memories. Her life goal is to help people make things better, one step at a time.

Kristine K. Nicholson has worked in multiple industries, the majority in healthcare operations, and focused on making things better everywhere she went. She earned her Bachelor of Science, Business - Healthcare Management and MBA, Healthcare Management degrees from Western

Governors University. She is a Certified Change Practitioner from Prosci, and Lean Black Belt and Lean Six Sigma green belt certified. She has been a guest on The

Lens podcast and was a presenter at Epic UGM (Users Group Meeting). She has a passion for learning, making things simple, and sharing for the benefit of others. Her influences include James Clear, author of Atomic Habits, Nedra Glover Tawwab, author of Find Boundaries, Find Peace, and Sharon McMahon, author of The Small and Mighty. Kristine has varied interests that include singing, painting, pickleball, laughing with friends and family, and meeting new people. Fun fact: She sang the Star-Spangled Banner opening for a Cheap Trick and Joan Jett concert at the Washington State Fair. She and her son, Chase, live in Maple Valley, Washington with a disco ball in the front window sparkling for all to see. Her life's mission is to spread joy like it's glitter.

SIMPLIFY

Simplify 98038 LLC

Website: https://The-Simple-Path.com

Email: info@the-simple-path.com

The SIMPLE Path Assessment

Rate yourself on the behaviors below.

0: Never	1: Rarely	2: Sometimes	3: Always

The SIMPLE Path	Behaviors	0	1	2	3
Start with you	I have a growth mindset.				
	I seek to understand.				
	I embrace change.				
Identify what is important	I know why my work matters.				
	I have a clear and concise direction.				
	I know who is impacted.				
Manage the chaos	I am able to eliminate distractions.				
	I create, communicate, and enforce boundaries.				
	I prioritize my attention on what I can control.				
Pick your improvement	I reduce complexity in everything I do.				
	I use evidence and data to understand what is really happening.				
	I consider the people who are impacted by the work.				

Learn from it	I avoid assumptions.				
	I embrace failure.				
	I use my learnings to implement or try again.				
Employ and enjoy	I communicate changes to those impacted.				
	I employ ways to make new ideas stick.				
	I celebrate the wins.				

Reflection:

- What sections are your strengths (highest scores)? How do you demonstrate these behaviors?

- What sections are your opportunities (lowest scores)? What section do you feel growth will make a difference in your life right now?

- What surprised you as you reflected on The SIMPLE Path and behaviors?

The SIMPLE Path Assessment

Rate yourself on the behaviors below.

0: Never	1: Rarely	2: Sometimes	3: Always

The SIMPLE Path	Behaviors	0	1	2	3
Start with you	I have a growth mindset.				
	I seek to understand.				
	I embrace change.				
Identify what is important	I know why my work matters.				
	I have a clear and concise direction.				
	I know who is impacted.				
Manage the chaos	I am able to eliminate distractions.				
	I create, communicate, and enforce boundaries.				
	I prioritize my attention on what I can control.				
Pick your improvement	I reduce complexity in everything I do.				
	I use evidence and data to understand what is really happening.				
	I consider the people who are impacted by the work.				

Learn from it	I avoid assumptions.				
	I embrace failure.				
	I use my learnings to implement or try again.				
Employ and enjoy	I communicate changes to those impacted.				
	I employ ways to make new ideas stick.				
	I celebrate the wins.				

Reflection:
- What sections are your strengths (highest scores)? How do you demonstrate these behaviors?

- What sections are your opportunities (lowest scores)? What section do you feel growth will make a difference in your life right now?

- What surprised you as you reflected on The SIMPLE Path and behaviors?

The SIMPLE Path Assessment

Rate yourself on the behaviors below.

0: Never	1: Rarely	2: Sometimes	3: Always

The SIMPLE Path	Behaviors	0	1	2	3
Start with you	I have a growth mindset.				
	I seek to understand.				
	I embrace change.				
Identify what is important	I know why my work matters.				
	I have a clear and concise direction.				
	I know who is impacted.				
Manage the chaos	I am able to eliminate distractions.				
	I create, communicate, and enforce boundaries.				
	I prioritize my attention on what I can control.				
Pick your improvement	I reduce complexity in everything I do.				
	I use evidence and data to understand what is really happening.				
	I consider the people who are impacted by the work.				

	I avoid assumptions.				
Learn from it	I embrace failure.				
	I use my learnings to implement or try again.				
	I communicate changes to those impacted.				
Employ and enjoy	I employ ways to make new ideas stick.				
	I celebrate the wins.				

Reflection:

- What sections are your strengths (highest scores)? How do you demonstrate these behaviors?

- What sections are your opportunities (lowest scores)? What section do you feel growth will make a difference in your life right now?

- What surprised you as you reflected on The SIMPLE Path and behaviors?

Start with you: I have a growth mindset.

How to Progress:
- Reflect every day.
- Apply a beginner's mind.
- Proactive thinking.

What will I commit to doing?

How can I start today?

Start with you: I seek to understand.

How to Progress:
- Start with positive intentions.
- Challenge your assumptions.
- Be curious.

What will I commit to doing?

How can I start today?

Start with you: I embrace change.

How to Progress:
- Try something new.
- Look for easier ways to do things.
- Understand your resistance.

What will I commit to doing?

How can I start today?

Identify what is important: I know why my work matters.

How to Progress:
- Create a mission statement.
- Create a vision statement.
- Share your elevator pitch.
- Be intentional.

What will I commit to doing?

How can I start today?

Identify what is important: I have a clear and concise direction.

How to Progress:
- Write SMARTIE goals and limit yourself to no more than 5.
- Make your goals visible.
- Review at least daily.

What will I commit to doing?

How can I start today?

Identify what is important: I know who is impacted.

How to Progress:
- Identify who your customers are.
- Ask your customers what they want/need.
- Understand who is involved.

What will I commit to doing?

How can I start today?

Manage the chaos: I am able to eliminate distractions.

How to Progress:
- Be present.
- Focus on what you can influence.
- Focus on one thing at a time.

What will I commit to doing?

How can I start today?

Manage the chaos: I create, communicate, and enforce boundaries.

How to Progress:
- Create boundaries.
- Craft a boundary statement.
- Create leader standard work.

What will I commit to doing?

How can I start today?

Manage the chaos: I prioritize my attention on what I can control.

How to Progress:

- Complete the MC Squares Exercise.

E = MC Squares

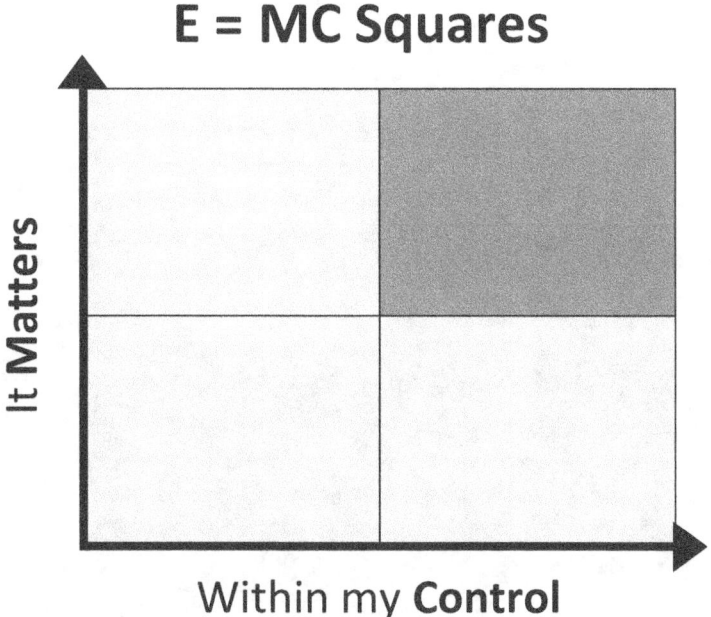

What will I commit to doing?

How can I start today?

Pick your improvement: I reduce complexity in everything I do.

How to Progress:
- Capture your current state.
- Develop a standard for one process.
- Measure what is important.
- Improve one thing at a time.

What will I commit to doing?

How can I start today?

Standard Process template

Step - Starts with a verb and is under 10 words.
Description - Description with pictures as needed of how to do the step.
Key Points - Why the step is needed and what could happen if not done a specific way.

Step	Description	Key Points

Improve one thing at a time template

What will you try?	What do you expect?	Try the thing	What happened?	What did you learn?

Pick your improvement: I use evidence and data to understand what is really happening.

How to Progress:
- Collect data.
- Challenge assumptions.
- Choose facts.

What will I commit to doing?

How can I start today?

Pick your improvement: I consider the people who are impacted by the work.

How to Progress:
- Defer to expertise.
- Reframe failure.
- Focus on the process rather than the outcome.

What will I commit to doing?

How can I start today?

Pick your improvement: I consider the people who are impacted by the work.

How to Progress:
- Defer to expertise.
- Reframe failure.
- Focus on the process rather than the outcome.

What will I commit to doing?

How can I start today?

Learn from it: I avoid assumptions.

How to Progress:
- Collect data to inform my learning.
- Add "because" after statements.

What will I commit to doing?

How can I start today?

Learn from it: I embrace failure.

How to Progress:
- Use "whoopsie" instead of "failure."
- Ask yourself, "What did I learn?"
- Add talking about a failure to a recurring agenda or conversation.

What will I commit to doing?

How can I start today?

Learn from it: I use my learnings to implement or try again.

How to Progress:
- Reflect on why things worked or didn't work.
- Reflect on a rapid improvement.
- Ask yourself, what did you learn from the last thing you tried?

What will I commit to doing?

How can I start today?

Employ and enjoy: I communicate changes to those impacted.

How to Progress:
- Inform those impacted by the change.
- Support people through change.

What will I commit to doing?

How can I start today?

Employ and enjoy: I employ ways to make new ideas stick.

How to Progress:
- Make it easy.
- Make it obvious.
- Find an accountability buddy.

What will I commit to doing?

How can I start today?

Employ and enjoy: I celebrate the wins.

How to Progress:
- Build in celebration.
- Make everyone part of the success.
- Show the data that demonstrates improvement.

What will I commit to doing?

How can I start today?

S I M P L I F Y

Simplify 98038 LLC

Website: https://The-Simple-Path.com

Email: info@the-simple-path.com

For additional support on your SIMPLE Path journey,
visit https://the-simple-path.com or email us at
info@the-simple-path.com to explore:
- Consultations for businesses and individuals
- One-on-one individual coaching
- Facilitated group workshops and retreats
- Supplemental Tools and Resources

We're here to walk alongside you—every step of the way.